Can You See Me?

by Ted Lewin

I Like to Read®

Holiday House / New York

We live in the rain forest.

I am a bird.
Can you see me?

I am a snake.
Can you see me?

I am a sloth.
Can you
see me?

I am a reptile.
Can you
see me?

I am an otter.
Can you see me?

I am a bird.
Can you
see me?

I am a monkey.
Can you see me?

I am a crab.
Can you see me?

I am a lizard.
I am hard to see.

I am a bird.
You will *never* see me.

I am a frog.
I am small,
but I am easy to see.

We are still here.

TOUCAN

VINE SNAKE

TWO-TOED SLOTH

SPECTACLED CAIMAN

RIVER OTTER

TIGER HERON

HOWLER MONKEY

LAND CRAB

BASILISK LIZARD

GREAT POTOO

RED POISON DART FROG